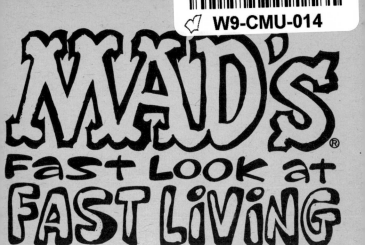

MAD'S FAST LOOK at FAST LIVING

Written by
Stan Hart
Illustrated by
Paul Coker, Jr.
Edited by
Nick Meglin

WARNER BOOKS

A Warner Communications Company

Contents

SCHOOL

In the future, colleges will have to keep pace with our fast living.

SPEED WRITING. Saturday 10:00 to 10:03 A.M.
In this course, the student is encouraged to write an original book at least as long as "Remembrances of Things Past" by Marcel Proust. Where it took Proust most of his life to write a work of such extraordinary length, the Lance Allworth University student learns the shortcuts that permit him to cut the writing time to less than an hour. Content not important.

SPEED CHAPEL. Sunday 9:00 to 9:01 A.M.
At L.A.U. we do not neglect religion, despite the hectic pace of the outside world. We take time out to reflect upon The Almighty in tranquility. The tranquility lasts all of 60 seconds. Perhaps 62 seconds, if there is a jam up at the exit.

SPEED GYM. Saturday 11:00 to 11:01 A.M.
At L.A.U. we feel the body is as important as the mind. Therefore, every student must spend at least part of a minute in Physical Education. There the student will do a push up, a jumping Jack, a sit up and finish off with a three yard dash.

SPEED CLASSICS Sunday 11:58 to lunch (Noon); and 3:00 to 3:03 P.M.
The morning session is an intensive course covering all the classic books ever written. The afternoon session covers all the other books that were ever written.

SPEED PHILOSOPHY, Sunday 4:05 to 4:07 P.M.

In this course, students will familiarize themselves with the great philosophies of The West and The East. The final exam will concern itself with such speed philosophy questions as, "Wsdagths?" and "Wds wreeees mrdalky?" Requisites: Speed Talking; Speed Listening.

SPEED MUSIC APPRECIATION Saturday 2:30 to 2:33 P.M.

Students will learn to appreciate the finer subtleties of the world's great music. The Minute Waltz (lasts 3 seconds) is analyzed and all nine Beethoven Symphonies are studied. The latter takes 45 seconds of class time. However, we believe in thoroughness when it comes to immortal music, which today might well take over an afternoon to create.

At Checker's A&M, you learn how to pack eggs on the bottom of the bag so they'll crush. How to make sure ice cream will leak and cause the bag to break in the parking lot. (See, it's not all work and no play, is it?) You will also learn techniques of overcharging and shortchanging and how to refuse to accept deposit bottles that belong to the store.

At Supers' Christian University, you learn how to keep warm during the winter while the tenants freeze their things off. You also learn how to hide from annoying tenants who make outrageous demands like asking to have the garbage picked up once a month or to have the lobby floor washed once a millennium.

FAST FOODS

You've all heard of *The Chain Of Life*, or *The Great Chain of Being*, or the phrase, "Chain of Events." If you haven't, I don't want to talk to you, 'cause you're an illiterate shmendrick who's screwing up my premise! Well, here's another chain—the fast food chain....

Advances in modern patent medicines... Fast
Relief...

Which leads to advances in bathroom livability.... Fast Air Fresheners...

...but dad can use it for a little around-the-house jobs, like puttying the windows. And the kids love mom's pudding, too. It can be molded into indestructible toy planes and tanks.

There you have it—a complete meal! The only things that had to be left out of the dinner were nutrition and flavor. It's a small price for getting Mom out of the kitchen fast so she can watch "Family Feud!"

TECHNOLOGY

The World of Technology is a wonderworld of electronic wizardry! For instance, years ago, there was no easy, cheap way of quickly duplicating 500 copies of a notice for your school dance. Today there is, thanks to Xerography!

Unfortunately, there's no easy, cheap or quick way to undo a spelling error on your 500 Xeroxed sheets, once they're printed.

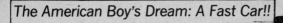
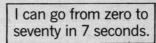

The old fashioned dial phone which once took almost eight seconds to dial a number, has been replaced by the Touch Tone Phone. It can get your number in 4½ seconds. That's a savings of 3½ seconds to goof around in. Think of it, if you used the Touch Tone and saved 3½ seconds and made 10 calls a day, seven days a week for ten years, you'd save 35 hours and be able to take over a day and a half vacation. On second thought, don't bother thinking of it.

*Which means, "Wong, is that you? Come on with your stupid Yankee impressions, already!"

TRAVEL

Sound fantastic? Well, it's true. On the Supersonic Transports, you can fly the Atlantic in less than four hours. Great? Sure. Only it's not *The Atlantic* that screws up your timing, it's getting to *The Atlantic* that does it. F'rinstance...

Thank you for being patient during our slight delay. We hope you will show the same cooperative spirit for our next delay which will be two hours. Thank you and have a nice day.

Enjoy running through historic places such as Parliament, The Tower of London and St. Paul's Cathedral. Lunch on The Underground on your way to Westminster Abbey. The morning concludes with a dash through Windsor Castle and connections to your tour bus that drives to the airport at breakneck speed. Shop at the cigar stand for a minute at Heathrow Airport, then all aboard for your flight to Paris.

Ah, what could be more romantic than Paris on a Wednesday afternoon? A squadron of motorcycle daredevils will meet you at the airport and whisk you to The Eiffel Tower where you will run up the stairs to the top, touch the Tower guard and run down again. Then on to Notre Dame Cathedral for a race through the aisles and off to Montmartre, where a speeding sight seeing bus will drive you through the artist's quarter at 80 miles an hour. Sit back and enjoy it. Then right out to the airport for your trip to Rome.

At the airport, you will be strapped to an intercontinental missile and shot to Rome. Travel time 35 minutes. While in the air, enjoy Southern France and parts of Switzerland. And then... Rome. The Eternal City. After you are dug out and unstrapped from your missile, you will be taken by ambulance (the only way to make time in Roman traffic) to The Via Veneto for window shopping on roller skates and off to the Coliseum for a minute visit (you can read all about the old crap when you get back home) and then the *piece de resistance*—a visit to The Vatican for a half blessing by The Pope.

And back to the airport to catch an SST home, thereby saving the high cost of a hotel room overnight. Just before midnight Wednesday, you're home. Isn't it grand to be back in the good old U.S. of A.?

COMMUNICATIONS

At the rate things are going, books will be shorter to allow for faster reading, such as...

This ad is irresistible to any 97 lb. weakling's 2½ lb. heart. With today's affluence, he can afford to send away for the course.

By the time summer comes around, he is no longer a scrawny 97 pounder but is now a 165 pound whopper.

Unfortunately, the sleazy advice you get only works on sleazy girls. Better you should read "Boy's Life" and instead of trying to make out with nice girls, help them untie any knots that might be bothering them.

Ever buy something from a mail order house? If you have, then you need not read further, you know the rest. If not.... (We're alone now, we can talk. Those idiots! Hah, hah, ha. Hey, shhhh, don't tell them we were laughing at them. Pretend like nothing happened when they rejoin us in two pages, okay? You're swell!)

Years ago, peoples' reputations were ruined by the slow spread of vicious gossip through whispering campaigns.

GOVERNMENT

Years ago, we had statesmen in the government. But today, we have fast talking politicians, talking fast-fixes for our problems...

I'll tell you why wage and price control can't work....
PRICES UP
EVEN MORE

Because gambling is such a big business, many State Governments want a piece of the action. So, they set up Off Track Betting Parlors.

The oodles of money The State makes goes to help the aged and the poor. Isn't that nice? And what do you think the aged and the poor do with the money they get?

107

In this case he pleaded guilty, not to the original crime of **homicide,** but to a lesser one of **Jay Walking!** He was fined $10 and warned to cross only at the corners!

MEDICINE

Today we have a wide spectrum of wonder drugs *that start to work almost instantly...*

So, our 50 year old woman has her eyes unwrinkled, her chin lifted and her tummy tucked. When she is finished, she won't look like an old bag anymore. However...

Since the bill is so huge (and not covered by any health insurance plan), she can't afford to buy new clothes. So, instead of looking like an old bag anymore, she now looks like a young bag!

On TV, drug companies claim you get fast relief from headaches with their tablets.

DAILY LIFE

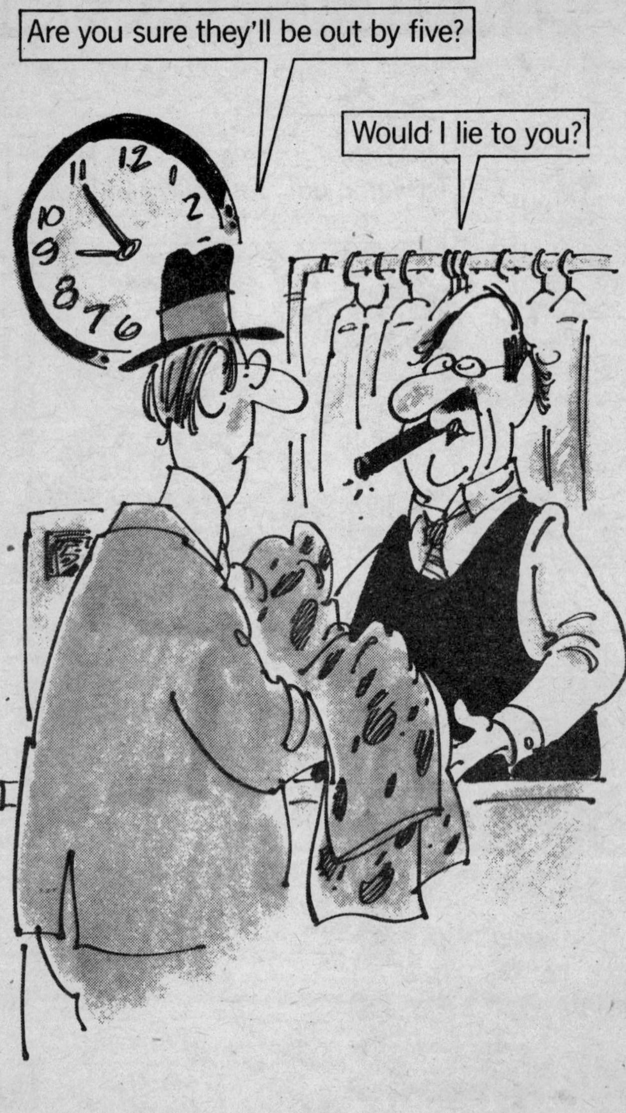
Are you sure they'll be out by five?
Would I lie to you?

133

140

Just call a plumber who advertises Fast Emergency Service. You say you don't trust the ad? Would he lie to you? Would a bear make **eng-eng** in the forest?

FAST MONEY

Unfortunately, "The Instant Cash Card" is also known as "The Instant Mugging Card."

157

The money a rock star makes is unimaginable. And the fame!! He's known, loved and sought after wherever he goes. 'Cause when you're hot, you're hot...

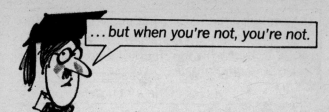

... but when you're not, you're not.

Hey out there, what say we go down Memory Lane and play an oldie? Ready for some nostalgia? See if you remember this guy. Hint... he was a big, big star way back about three weeks ago....

161

"Oh, no," you cry? "Oh, yes," cries back the kindly old gentleman with the whiskers and funky hat. Where are you going to get the money to pay? Well, you just went through Phase One: Buy! Buy!! Buy!!! Now, it's Phase Two: Sell! Sell!! Sell!!!

...the accountant's ledger reads...

While, on the **other** side of the Ledger...

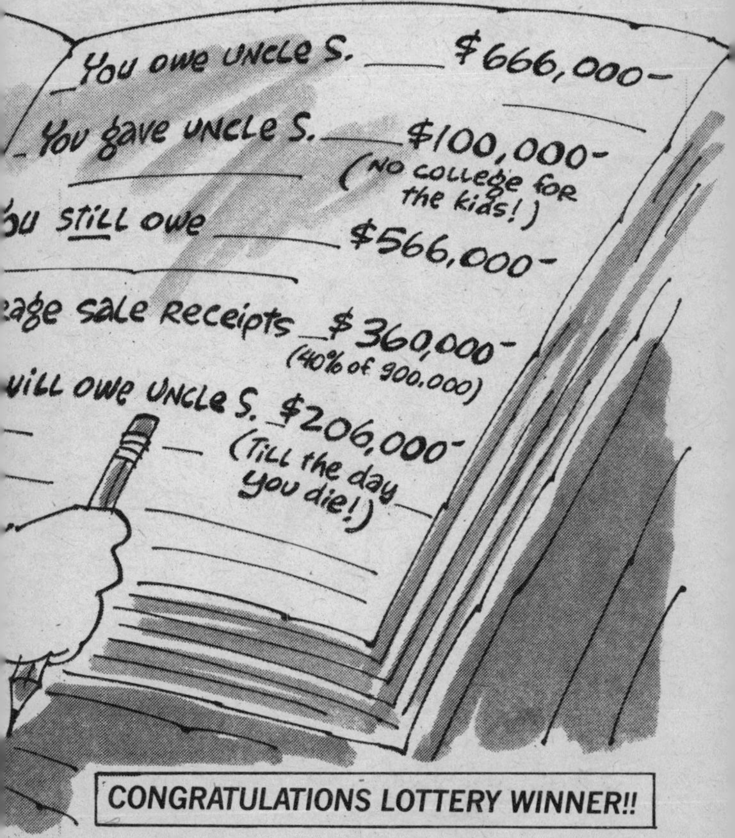

CONGRATULATIONS LOTTERY WINNER!!

TELEVISION

Remember years ago, before TV news became the most important way to give information, there was a thing called "A Newspaper"? Nice sound…"Newspaper." Well, in this thing called "A Newspaper" was something called a Theater Critic. It was a man who knew what he was watching when he went to the theater. He would see a play, then go back to the office and write a criticism of the play he had just seen. It took him an hour or more to write a thoughtful review. But now, thanks to INSTANT JOURNALISM on TV, we get theater criticism without having to wait…

The theater critic, who used to do the weather, but did it badly and had to find something else to do, rushes in for his one minute review...

How did he really like the play? Who knows? He never saw it. He was in a bar, next to the theater, getting fried. His review? He asked a bag lady who had been in the theater getting warm how she liked it. She hasn't liked anything since her pet roach died.

Another improvement! Now you don't have to get out of your seat in order to change the channel…

PLINK
FOIMP
PLOINK
GLINK

Of course you can change channels, but you still won't find a program worth watching. Wait until they perfect UHF and you have 100 stations. You'll spend half the night switching around to find something to watch—and you'll still be disappointed.

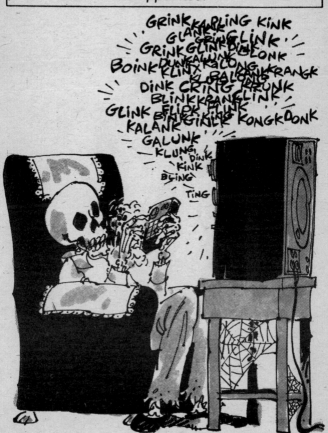

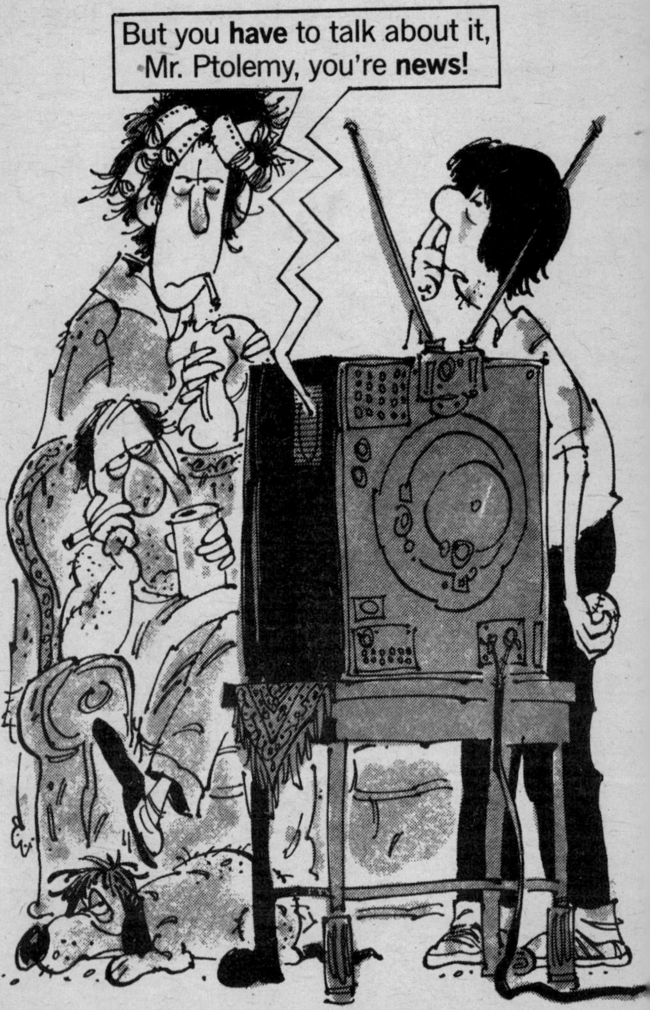
But you **have** to talk about it, Mr. Ptolemy, you're **news**!